Families

Aunts and Uncles

Rebecca Rissman

www.raintreepublishers.co.uk
Visit our website to find out more information about Raintree books.

To order:
☎ Phone 0845 6044371
🖹 Fax +44 (0) 1865 312263
🖳 Email myorders@raintreepublishers.co.uk

Customers from outside the UK please telephone +44 1865 312262

Raintree is an imprint of Capstone Global Library Limited, a company incorporated in England and Wales having its registered office at 7 Pilgrim Street, London, EC4V 6LB – Registered company number: 6695582

Edited by Rebecca Rissman, Dan Nunn, and Catherine Veitch
Designed by Ryan Frieson
Picture research by Tracy Cummins
Production by Victoria Fitzgerald
Originated by Capstone Global Library
Printed and bound in China by Leo Paper Products Ltd

ISBN 978 1 406 22151 0
14 13 12 11 10
10 9 8 7 6 5 4 3 2 1

British Library Cataloguing in Publication Data
Rissman, Rebecca.
Aunts and uncles. -- (Families)
306.8'7-dc22

Acknowledgements
We would like to thank the following for permission to reproduce photographs: Corbis pp. **12** (©Larry Williams), **16** (©Tim Pannell), **17** (©Rick Gomez), **18** (©Tim Pannell), **19** (©A. Chederros/Onoky), **23 d** (©Larry Williams); Getty images pp. **4** (Henrik Sorensen), **5** (Eri Morita), **6** (Michael Hall), **9** (Betsie Van der Meer), **10** (Henrik Trygg), **11** (Blend Images/ JR Carvey/Streetfly Studio), **13** (Apple Tree House), **14** (David Sacks), **15** (Blend Images/Jon Feingersh), **20** (Loungepark), **21** (flashfilm), **23 a** (Blend Images/JR Carvey/Streetfly Studio), **23 b** (Loungepark), **23 c** (Eri Morita); istockphoto pp. **8** (©TriggerPhoto), **22** (©Diane Labombarbe); Shutterstock p. **7** (©Kacso Sandor).

Front cover photograph of a family walking in the park reproduced with permission of Getty Images (Ronnie Kaufman). Back cover photograph of aunts and uncles reproduced with permission of Corbis (©Larry Williams).

We would like to thank Anne Pezalla, Dee Reid and Diana Bentley for their invaluable help in the preparation of this book.

Every effort has been made to contact copyright holders of material reproduced in this book. Any omissions will be rectified in subsequent printings if notice is given to the publisher.

Contents

What is a family?

A family is a group of people who care for each other.

People in a family are called
family members.

All families are different.

All families are special.

What are families like?

Families can be big or small.

Families enjoy doing things together.

Who are aunts and uncles?

Some families have aunts and uncles.

Aunts and uncles are your parents'
sisters and brothers.

Your parent's sister is your aunt.
Your parent's brother is your uncle.

Some families call special friends
aunts and uncles.

Different aunts and uncles

Some families have many aunts
and uncles.

Some families have few aunts and uncles. Some families have none.

Some people's aunts and uncles live with them.

Some people's aunts and uncles live
far away.

Some aunts and uncles are young.
Some aunts and uncles are old.

Some aunts and uncles have children of their own.

If your aunts and uncles have children, they are your cousins.

Do you have aunts and uncles?

Family tree

Grandmother — Grandfather

Aunt — Uncle Your Parent Aunt — Uncle

You

Picture glossary

 **aunt** a parent's sister

 **cousin** child of an aunt or uncle

 **member** person who belongs to a group

 **uncle** a parent's brother

Index

Note to parents and teachers

Before reading

Ask children to name different people who can be in a family (e.g. parents, grandparents, brothers, sisters, cousins). Record their answers in a list on the board. Then ask children if they know who aunts and uncles are, and how they can be related to their families. Explain that aunts and uncles are usually the sisters and brothers of parents.

After reading

After reviewing the family tree on page 22, encourage children to draw their own family tree. If they have aunts and uncles, help the children to include them on their family tree.